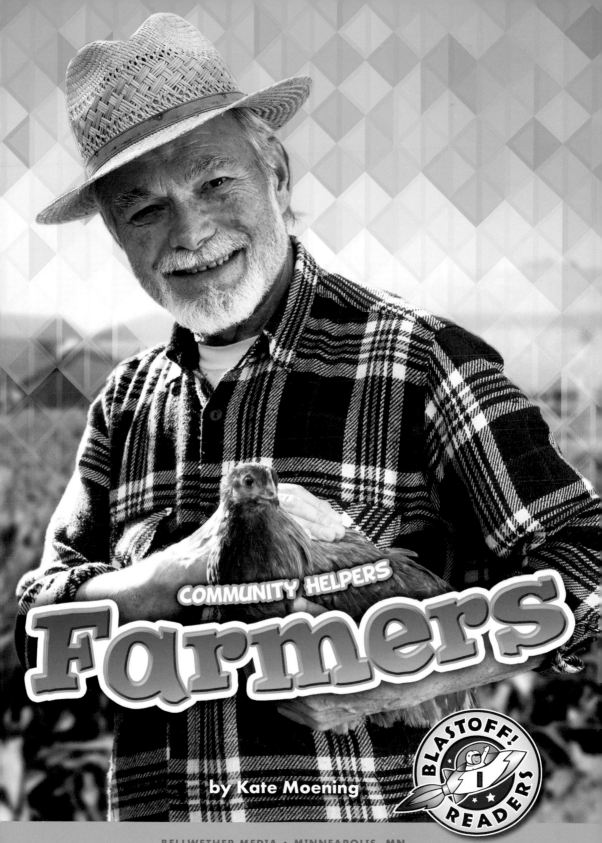

COMMUNITY HELPERS

Farmers

by Kate Moening

BLASTOFF!
READERS

BELLWETHER MEDIA • MINNEAPOLIS, MN

Note to Librarians, Teachers, and Parents:

Blastoff! Readers are carefully developed by literacy experts and combine standards-based content with developmentally appropriate text.

Level 1 provides the most support through repetition of high-frequency words, light text, predictable sentence patterns, and strong visual support.

Level 2 offers early readers a bit more challenge through varied simple sentences, increased text load, and less repetition of high-frequency words.

Level 3 advances early-fluent readers toward fluency through increased text and concept load, less reliance on visuals, longer sentences, and more literary language.

Level 4 builds reading stamina by providing more text per page, increased use of punctuation, greater variation in sentence patterns, and increasingly challenging vocabulary.

Level 5 encourages children to move from "learning to read" to "reading to learn" by providing even more text, varied writing styles, and less familiar topics.

Whichever book is right for your reader, Blastoff! Readers are the perfect books to build confidence and encourage a love of reading that will last a lifetime!

This edition first published in 2019 by Bellwether Media, Inc.

No part of this publication may be reproduced in whole or in part without written permission of the publisher. For information regarding permission, write to Bellwether Media, Inc., Attention: Permissions Department, 6012 Blue Circle Drive, Minnetonka, MN 55343.

Library of Congress Cataloging-in-Publication Data

Names: Moening, Kate, author.
Title: Farmers / by Kate Moening.
Description: Minneapolis, MN : Bellwether Media, Inc., 2019. | Series:
  Blastoff! Readers. Community Helpers | Includes bibliographical references
  and index.
Identifiers: LCCN 2017057277 (print) | LCCN 2017058877 (ebook) | ISBN
  9781626178977 (hardcover : alk. paper) | ISBN 9781681035345 (ebook)
Subjects: LCSH: Farmers–Juvenile literature.
Classification: LCC S519 (ebook) | LCC S519 .M678 2019 (print) | DDC
  630.92–dc23
LC record available at https://lccn.loc.gov/2017057277

Editor: Christina Leaf   Designer: Brittany McIntosh

Printed in the United States of America, North Mankato, MN.

Table of Contents

Looking After Animals

It is morning on the farm. The farmer gathers eggs from the chickens.

Next, she checks
on the cows.
A farmer's work
is never done!

What Are Farmers?

Farmers supply our food! They grow **crops** and raise **livestock**.

Most farms are in the **countryside**, but some are in cities and towns.

What Do Farmers Do?

Many farmers care for livestock.
They gather goods like milk and eggs.

Other farmers grow
and **harvest** crops.
Tools like tractors
and **plows** help
with tasks.

tractor

Farmer Gear

tractor   plow   seeds   animal feed

Crops need the right weather to grow. Farmers keep track of the **seasons**.

What Makes a Good Farmer?

Crops and animals have many needs. Farmers fix problems they have to keep them healthy.

Farmer Skills

✓ problem-solvers   ✓ careful

✓ good with machines   ✓ strong

Farmers must be hard workers. They are ready to go, rain or shine!

Glossary

countryside

land outside of cities or towns

livestock

animals raised for human use, usually for food, clothing, or work

crops

plants grown for people to use

plows

machines that turn over soil for planting

harvest

to gather crops when they are ripe

seasons

times of year with certain types of weather; spring, summer, fall, and winter are the four seasons.

To Learn More

AT THE LIBRARY

Borth, Teddy. *Life on the Farm*. Minneapolis, Minn.: Abdo Kids, 2015.

Dobbins, Jan. *A Farmer's Life for Me*. Cambridge, Mass.: Barefoot Books, 2013.

Liebman, Daniel. *I Want to Be a Farmer*. Richmond Hill, Ont.: Firefly Books, 2016.

ON THE WEB

Learning more about farmers is as easy as 1, 2, 3.

1. Go to www.factsurfer.com.

2. Enter "farmers" into the search box.

3. Click the "Surf" button and you will see a list of related web sites.

With factsurfer.com, finding more information is just a click away.

Index

The images in this book are reproduced through the courtesy of: Alexander Raths, front cover; MaxyM, pp. 2-3; bernatets photo, pp. 4-5, 6-7; Monkey Business Images, pp. 8-9; Sarine Arslanian, pp. 10-11; Ariel Skelley/ Alamy, pp. 12-13; oticki, pp. 14-15, 22 (crops); Bjorn Heller, p. 15 (tractor); arogant, p. 15 (plow); Andris Tkacenko, p. 15 (seeds); domnitsky, p. 15 (animal feed); Pradana, pp. 16-17; Dipak Shelare, pp. 18-19; Ron_Thomas, pp. 20-21; Kevin Eaves, p. 22 (countryside); Steve Heap, p. 22 (harvest); Sara Winter, p. 22 (livestock); tanger, p. 22 (plows); Hannamariah, p. 22 (seasons).